R

B L O O M S B U R Y
LONDON · NEW DELHI · NEW YORK · SYDNEY

Bloomsbury Methuen Drama

An imprint of Bloomsbury Publishing Plc

50 Bedford Square	1385 Broadway
London	New York
WC1B 3DP	NY 10018
UK	USA

www.bloomsbury.com

Bloomsbury is a registered trade mark of Bloomsbury Publishing Plc

First published 2014

© Rachel De-lahay, 2014

Rachel De-lahay has asserted her right under
the Copyright, Designs and Patents Act 1988
to be identified as the author of this work.

British Library Cataloguing-in-Publication Data

A catalogue record for this book is available from the British Library

ISBN: PB: 978-1-4725-9191-3
ePub: 978-1-4725-9192-0
ePDF: 978-1-4725-9193-7

Library of Congress Cataloging-in-Publication Data

A catalog record for this book is available from the Library of Congress.

Typeset by Country Setting, Kingsdown, Kent CT14 8ES
Printed and bound in Great Britain

BIRMINGHAM REPERTORY THEATRE COMPANY

presents

CIRCLES
by Rachel De-lahay

Circles received its first performance at Birmingham Repertory
Theatre on 9 May 2014

Malachi	Toyin Kinch
Angela	Sarah Manners
Phyllis	Janice McKenzie
Demi	Danusia Samal

Director	Tessa Walker
Designer	Bob Bailey
Lighting Designer	Simon Bond
Sound Designer	Becky Smith
Casting Director	Polly Jerrold
Movement Director	Anna Morrissey
Fight Director	Renny Krupinski
Production Manager	Sara Crathorne
Stage Manager	Michael Ramsay
Deputy Stage Manager	Amber Curtis

CAST

Toyin Kinch
Theatre credits include: *At The Gates Of Gaza* (Birmingham Repertory Theatre); *Marcus Da Sadist* (Jonzi D Productions); *Not Quite Gospel* (Nu Century Arts); *The Lost Happy Endings* (mac Birmingham/Red Earth Theatre); *The Day the Waters Came* (Theatre Centre) and *The Flying Machine* (The Unicorn). Film and television credits include: *The Games Men Play* (B19 Media); *The Door* (Soap Box/Creative Partnerships) and *Doctors* (BBC).

Sarah Manners
Television credits include: *The Job Lot* (Big Talk); *The Bill* (Talkback Thames); *Casualty* and *Doctors* (BBC) and *Mile High* (Sky 1). Film credits include: *Beginner's Luck* (Late Night Films) and *Sugar Sugar* (Sweet Tooth Films). Theatre credits include: *Survive* (New Alexandra Theatre), *The Watcher* (Waterloo East Theatre), *The Decorator* (national tour) and *Communicating Doors* (Chester Gateway Theatre).

Janice McKenzie
Television credits include: *Family Affairs* (Grundy Productions); *Emmerdale* and *The Royal* (Yorkshire TV) and *Heartbeat* (ITV Yorkshire). Theatre credits include: *Spring Storm* (National Theatre), *Noises Off*, *Antony And Cleopatra*, *Hobson's Choice* and *These Four Streets* (Birmingham Repertory Theatre); *Henry V* (Royal Shakespeare Company) and *The Prime of Miss Jean Brodie* and *One Flew over the Cuckoo's Nest* (New Vic).

Danusia Samal
Theatre credits include: *Billy the Girl* (Clean Break/Soho Theatre); *Finding Noor* (Citizens Theatre); *The Birthday Party* (Manchester Royal Exchange); *Liar, Liar* and *1001 Nights* (Unicorn Theatre); *After the Rainfall* (Curious Directive); *Water Under The Bridge* (White Bear Theatre) and *Street Scene* and *The Suit* (Young Vic).

CREATIVE TEAM

Rachel De-lahay Writer
Rachel's first play *The Westbridge* went on to win the 2012
Writers' Guild Award for best play as well as coming joint first for
the 2011 Alfred Fagan Award. Her second play, *Routes*, was at
the Royal Court in September 2013. Rachel is currently
developing her first feature with Film Four and Independent
Films and won the Pearson Award to write for Birmingham
Repertory Theatre in 2013.

Tessa Walker Director
Tessa is an Associate Director at Birmingham Repertory Theatre.
She has previously been the Literary Director at Paines Plough
and a Literary Associate at the National Theatre of Scotland. Her
credits include: *A Christmas Carol* and *The Mother* (Birmingham
Repertory Theatre); *The Gatekeeper* (Manchester Royal
Exchange); *Dream Pill* and *Dancing Bears* (Clean Break, Soho
Theatre) and *The Kitchen Sink* (Hull Truck).

Bob Bailey Designer
Bob trained at Central St Martin's College of Art and Design,
London. His credits include: *The Empire* and *The Lying Kind* (Royal
Court); *Translations* and *Moll Flanders* (Bristol Old Vic); *The
Woman In Black* (Vienna); *Solid Air* (Plymouth Drum); *The
Santaland Diaries* (Birmingham Repertory Theatre). Dance credits
include: *All Nighter* and *Horse-Play* (Royal Ballet) and *The
Happiest Day of My Life* (set design only, for DV8 Physical
Theatre Company: UK/European tour), for which Bob was
awarded *Time Out* Designer of the Year.

Simon Bond Lighting Designer
Simon is a Lighting Technician at Birmingham Repertory Theatre.
Recent designs include: *Respect, Cling To Me Like Ivy, 8sixteen32,
Looking For Yoghurt, Notes To Future Self, The Importance Of
Being Earnest, Travesties, Gravity, The Legend Of Mike Smith,
Hopelessly Devoted* and *Europa*.

Becky Smith Sound Designer
Becky studied drama at Exeter University and has worked as stage manager for companies including ATC, Paines Plough, The Gate, Polka Theatre and Oily Cart. Her sound designs include: *Frozen* (Fingersmiths/Birmingham Repertory Theatre); *Billy the Girl*, *A Just Act*, *This Wide Night* and *Missing Out* (Clean Break); *Bird*, *Lagan* (Root Theatre); *The Kitchen Sink* (Hull Truck); *Brood* (Stratford East); and *The Juniper Tree*, *Reverence* and *The Ghost Sonata* (Goat and Monkey).

Polly Jerrold Casting Director
This is the second production that Polly has cast for The REP, having worked with Tessa Walker on Bryony Lavery's adaptation of *A Christmas Carol* in 2013. Prior to this Polly was the Casting Associate at the Royal Exchange Theatre for five years, where she worked on an extensive and eclectic range of productions from the world premiere of Simon Stephens' *Punk Rock* to Bernstein's *Wonderful Town* in association with the Hallé Orchestra under Sir Mark Elder. Most recently she cast Ostrovsky's *Too Clever by Half* for Told by an Idiot, for whom she is now a board member. Polly has worked on lots of new writing including works by Chloe Moss, Alistair McDowall, Rory Mullarkey, Vivienne Franzmann, Janice Okoh and Tom Wells, whose play *The Kitchen Sink* she worked on with Tessa again, this time for Hull Truck Theatre. Polly also holds a number of workshops for Ideas Tap and is currently supporting the Andrew Scott mentoring scheme.

Anna Morrissey Movement Director
Anna's movement and choreography credits include *Charles III* (Almeida); *A Christmas Carol* (Birmingham Repertory Theatre); *The World of Extreme Happiness* (National Theatre); *Pericles*, *Marat/Sade*, *Antony and Cleopatra*, *The Grain Store*, *The Drunks* (Royal Shakespeare Company); *Macbeth*, *The Flying Dutchman* and *Noyes Fludde* (NI Opera); *Dunsinane* (National Theatre of Scotland) and the London 2012 Olympic Opening Ceremony (Movement Assistant). Anna is currently Artist in Residence for Historic Royal Palaces.

BIRMINGHAM REPERTORY THEATRE COMPANY

Development Manager
Anya Sampson

Development Officers
Ros Adams
Rachel Cranny

Development Assistant
Alana Tomlin

Project Producer
Jenny Smith

Theatre Sales Manager
Gerard Swift

Assistant Theatre & Sales Managers
James Dakers
Rachel Foster
Kieran Johnson
Maria Kavalieros

Theatre & Sales Assistants
Anne Bower
Fran Esposito
Robert Flynn
Matt Jukes
Sebastian Maynard-Francis
Eileen Minnock
Carla Smith
Rhys Worgan

Theatre Operations Manager
Nigel Cairns

Theatre Shop Supervisor
Grace Page

Theatre Cleaning Supervisors
Jane Browning
Suri Matoo

Theatre Cleaning Assistants
Samantha Clarke
Neville Claxton
Debra Cuthill
Ilyas Fareed
Kenny Ibrahim
Rebecca McDonald
Naomi Minnen
Tracey O'Dell

Head of Production
Tomas Wright

Production Manager
Milorad Žakula

Production Assistant
Laura Killeen

Company Manager
Ruth Morgan

Head of Wardrobe
Sue Nightingale

Costume Cutters & Makers
Fiona Mills
Kay Wilton

Head of Wigs & Make-up
Andrew Whiteoak

Head of Lighting
Andrew Fidgeon

Senior Technician (Lighting)
Simon Bond

Technician (Lighting)
Liam Jones

Head of Sound & AV
Dan Hoole

Senior Technician (Sound & AV)
Clive Meldrum

Head Scenic Artist
Christopher Tait

Design Manager
Olly Shapley

Head of Scenery & Props
Margaret Rees

Senior Scenic Maker
Simon Fox

Scenic Makers
Laura Davies
Amy Passey

Technical Co-ordinator
Adrian Bradley

Building Maintenance Technician
Leon Gatenby

Technicians (Stage)
Ross Gallagher
Laurel Griffiths
Kieren Keogh

**With thanks to all our Front of House
Theatre Assistants, Stage Crew and
Volunteers**

BIRMINGHAM REPERTORY THEATRE

Birmingham Repertory Theatre is one of Britain's leading producing theatre companies. Founded in 1913 by Sir Barry Jackson, Birmingham Repertory Theatre Company rapidly became one of the most famous and exciting theatre companies in the country, launching the careers of an array of great British actors, including Laurence Olivier, Ralph Richardson, Edith Evans, Paul Scofield, Derek Jacobi, Elizabeth Spriggs, Albert Finney and many more. In 2013 the company celebrated its centenary.

The theatre's programme includes many premieres, from new versions of the classics to contemporary writing. The commissioning and production of new work lies at the core of The REP's programme and over the last 15 years the company has produced more than 130 new plays.

Many of The REP's productions go on to have lives beyond Birmingham, transferring to the West End and touring nationally and internationally. Recent transfers and tours include *Twelve Angry Men* at the Garrick Theatre, Philip Pullman's *I Was A Rat!* and Kate Tempest's *Hopelessly Devoted*.

The REP's long-running production of *The Snowman* recently celebrated its twentieth anniversary. It has become a must-see fixture in London's West End calendar, playing to packed houses at the Peacock Theatre every Christmas for the last fifteen years. *The Snowman* also tours regularly across the UK and to theatres in Holland, Korea, Japan and Finland.

The REP reopened in Autumn 2013 following a two-and-a-half-year refurbishment alongside the new Library of Birmingham. The refurbishment of the theatre includes a new 300-seat studio theatre as well as the restoration of its original façade, plus much improved public and backstage facilities

Artistic Director Roxana Silbert
Executive Director Stuart Rogers

Box Office 0121 236 4455 | Administration: 0121 245 2000
birmingham-rep.co.uk

Birmingham Repertory Theatre is a registered charity, number 223660

This production has been supported by

Circles

Characters

Phyllis, *fifties*
Angela, *thirties*
Demi, *fifteen*
Malachi, *sixteen*

Location

Birmingham. We're either on the top deck of the No. 11 bus or in the living room of a two-up, two-down terrace house.

Two moveable benches represent bus seats and a home sofa.

Scene One

Malachi *is sitting at the back of the No. 11 bus.* **Demi** *is further forward.* **Malachi** *is talking loudly into his mobile phone.*

Malachi Oi fam! Nah! I told you outsides McDonald's on the ramp, innit? Tubz! No one told you to take farce and go Bullring!

What? Gal? Who? That one from Footlocker?! Ah, I beg you ask if she can hook me up with discount. True say pennies are tight whilst I'm saving up for my S3! Ya get me, fam?!

Just ask her!

I'm ra on the bus right now, going wiz-erk! Serious! Car's in the garage still. Man talking about effed clutch or some shit like that! And I ra know it's the gear-linkage! Trying to take mans for an eediot. But he can carry on still! True say he's my man's dad, I'll just 'low him! Otherwise you know I'd be carrying on militant! He'd have had to be boyed up, fam! Standard! Innit?!

Ah, that ting! Nah, she was on me still. Belling off my phone like it's a hot line!

Nah, I tapped it still! Standard! Gal could hardly walk, bredrin! Screaming down the place. I had to tell her to shush, ya get me? Mans like me got neighbours! And Tubz, this will give you joke –

His phone rings. He momentarily freezes before answering quickly and speaking quietly.

Hello?

Mom? Yeah, yeah. Nah, it's in the fridge. In a margarine tub.

No, I left enough for you and Dean in the microwave, covered with a plate. Cool? Yeah, yeah, finish normal time. I'll be back to take him to school, alright?

Safe. Night.

Love you too.

Malachi *hangs up.* **Demi** *turns around to look at him.*

Malachi   What?!

She turns back round, smiling to herself. **Malachi** *rolls his eyes and sighs. Lights fade.*

Scene Two

Phyllis *is sitting in an armchair.* **Angela** *is standing, carrying a small overnight bag. Her eye is bruised and lip cut.*

Beat.

Phyllis   Hiya, love.

Angela   Hiya, Mom.

Phyllis   You're out and about late.

Angela   I was just passing and saw your light on. Thought I'd say hey.

Phyllis   Nice.

Angela   I did try the bell but . . .

Phyllis   It died. A while back. Phone didn't though, if people needed me.

Beat.

So, how have you been?

Angela   Not bad. Really. Yourself?

Phyllis   Oh, you know me. Surviving.

Angela   Good.

Phyllis   You've changed your hair.

Angela   No.

Phyllis   I mean you have . . .

Angela   Oh, this hair? Yeah . . . Yes. I dyed it back. The blonde was getting expensive. The maintenance and that.

Phyllis   I said it would, didn't I? I said. Every four weeks? It adds up.

Angela   . . . You did.

Phyllis   And you've lost weight.

Angela   No.

Phyllis   It's not a bad thing.

Angela   I know.

Phyllis   No need to get defensive.

Angela   I'm not.

Phyllis   Good.

You look . . . good.

Beat.

Here! See what I picked up down the market the other week. Four ninety-nine.

Phyllis *reveals a plastic grabber.*

Angela   Your back still playing up?

Phyllis   This is amazing. Chuck your bag down. In front of me, here.

Go on.

Angela *places her overnight bag on the floor.* **Phyllis** *attempts to reach for it with the tool.*

Phyllis   Hang on.

Hang on.

Kick it forward a bit.

Angela *kicks the bag slightly towards* **Phyllis**, *who finally reaches the bag and lifts it up like a prize.*

Phyllis   See?

Angela   . . . Great.

Phyllis   Reckon the doctors should have prescribed me this all them years ago instead of all them drugs.

Angela   You shouldn't stop bending just 'cause it hurts.

Phyllis   You shouldn't stop doing a lot of things 'cause they hurt, but still people do. And for four ninety-nine, if I don't have to bend, I won't.

Angela   Well, that sounds smart. Like a smart decision.

Phyllis   And look here! You're gonna love these, you are.

She kicks her leg out to display her shoe.

Angela   New?

Phyllis   Got them re-soled. Found a special cobbler, right at the back of the market. See the sole on that one.

Angela   It's bigger.

Phyllis   I know. He reckons he can do it on all my shoes as well. For my limp, you know? So good. Found him in on Google.

Angela   That's . . .

I'm gonna pop this in the attic.

Phyllis   You're staying then?

Angela   Well, it's late, and I'm in the area . . .

Phyllis   With your stuff.

Angela   With some stuff, yes.

Phyllis   And Demi?

Angela   It's late, Mom.

Phyllis It would have been good to see her.

Angela And a school night so . . .

Phyllis So you left her? I hear ya.

Angela It's just one night.

Phyllis Sounds smart. Like a smart decision.

She takes a prescribed painkiller.

Like mother like daughter after all, eh?

Angela Despite all my prayers.

Phyllis As long as you're praying for the right thing.

I'll pop kettle on.

She exits, leaving **Angela** *still standing with her bag.*

Scene Three

Malachi *walks down the aisle of the bus talking loudly on his mobile phone.*

Malachi Tubz! Nah. Bredrin! I'm telling you that girl's an eediot! Tubz! She was chatting shit! She's not on my level, blood! Yeah yeah . . . yeah . . .

Noticing **Demi**, **Malachi** *quickly hides his phone and then takes a seat behind her.* **Demi** *pretends not to have noticed.*

Malachi Oi.

Oi!

Don't carry on like you're too stoosh. Oi!

Gal!

He gets up and moves closer to where **Demi** *is sitting.*

Malachi You hard of hearing?

Demi   I'm sorry?

Malachi   You not hear me calling you?

Demi   Oh, you were calling me? Sorry, I thought you were on the phone. It's hard to tell with you.

Malachi   Funny. Yo, pop your number in there for me, please?

Demi   Excuse me?

Malachi   Hang on a sec . . . 0 . . . 7 . . . 9 . . . ?

Demi   Er . . . nah, soz, mate.

Malachi   Why are you even fronting for? You've been sharking me since I walked up the stairs.

Demi   Really? That's odd since you're not even my type.

Malachi   What? 'Handsome' not your type?

Demi   Pedestrians aren't my type.

Malachi   And what are you driving? Let me guess . . . Giving the X5 a break today, are we?

Demi   I'm guessing it's in the same place as your S3.

Malachi   Slipping! What you doing listening to big man's conversations for?

Demi   Big what? Oh, I get it, you're a comedian. Yeah, why don't you and your school uniform move up!

Malachi   School uniform? Sweetheart. I'm a worker. Don't get it twisted. I'm a big man to you, ya get me?!

Demi   Why? 'Cause you have to babysit your brother . . . ? And Mom by the seems of it.

Malachi   Don't think 'cause you're a girl I won't kick you in your mouth!

Demi   . . . I'm guessing you're not wanting the number any more.

Beat.

Malachi   So where is your man?

Demi   At home.

Malachi   Waiting for you?

Demi   Yes.

Malachi   And you don't deal with mans that walk, so he must drive, right?

Demi   Right.

Malachi   What car?

Demi   A Mini Cooper S, in gunmetal, with the black roof.

Malachi   Yeah? My cousin Tubz has got that car, still. But in red.

Demi   Wow-ee!

Malachi   That not sting?

Demi   What?

Malachi   Knowing your man's driving a Mini Cooper S with the black roof thingy and yet you still have to catch the bus!

Demi   I'm an independent woman. I don't need no man to pick me up or drop me off no place.

Malachi   Course not!

Don't try pull that Beyoncé shit on me! You ain't got no man, you ain't got no car, your monthly bus pass comes with a student discount and you think you're better than me?

Demi   Finally. It seems we're on the same page.

Malachi   You know what? 'Low you, man.

He turns to move seats.

Demi   What? Not used to girls who can keep up with you?

Malachi   Keep up with what?

Demi   I know what you're about already. Absolute galis! And I bet I can guess your type in a second. Pretty face, nice smile, can match her lip-gloss to her nail varnish perfectly but ask her how to get to Birmingham Library and she'll go blank, right?

Malachi   Nah. That ain't my type. Don't get me wrong, I'd bang it, still, but now someone like you's more my type.

Demi   Me? Why, 'cause I'm intriguing?

Malachi   Maybe.

Demi   'Cause I'm here?

Malachi   Possibly.

Demi   'Cause I'm light-skinned?

Malachi   . . .

Demi   You know fuck-all about me.

Malachi   Oh my days! Did you just swear?!

You're right! I don't know nothing about you! I never would have put you down for a swearer! You look so smart.

Demi   I am.

Malachi   Please! Educated people don't swear.

Demi   I just wanted to make sure you understood me so I'm trying to speak to you on your level.

Malachi *notices his friend outside and is instantly distracted.*

Malachi (*through the window*)   Oi! Oi! 'Bout ya eating Papa Johns, ya tramp! And you call yourself a Muslim?! Joka!

Huh?! I can't hear ya! Bell me, fam!

He leaves the window and comes back to **Demi**.

Malachi   What school did you say you went to?

Demi   I didn't.

Malachi   Fine. What school do you go to?

Demi   Swanshurst.

Malachi   What kind of foreign school's that? That even in Brum?

Demi   Yes. It's a girls' school.

Malachi   Ah seen. What's your name?

Demi   . . . Demi.

Malachi   Like Demi Moore?

Demi   I guess.

Malachi   Moore. Gimme more. Gimme gimme more. I'm Malachi.

Demi   I know.

Malachi   Huh?

Demi   As I said, I'm smart. And one step ahead of you already.

Malachi *smiles.*

Blackout.

Scene Four

Phyllis *enters.* **Angela** *is curled up on the sofa nursing a tea.*

Phyllis   What the hell is going on? It's like a teenager's bedroom in here!

Angela   Huh?

Phyllis   Sheila said the curtains have been closed all day. You don't open curtains in your house?

Angela   It's night now. Unless you want me to . . .

She makes to open the curtains.

Phyllis   Don't try and get smart.

Angela   It's one day. And they're only curtains. And what even happens if you don't open them? Nothing.

Phyllis   People think you've died. About nothing! Sheila would have thought I was dead.

Angela   From the curtains –

Phyllis   From the curtains being closed, yes. All day? That's a house in mourning.

Beat.

Angela   She didn't knock on.

Phyllis   What?

Angela   If she thought you'd died.

She never knocked on, to check, or offer condolences or anything. No one did. All day.

Phyllis   OK. You want to sulk. If that's where you're at . . .

And I wouldn't have answered, would I? If I was dead. So it would have been a waste of time anyone trying to knock on. And they would have known that. Sheila would have known that, so . . .

Angela   . . . There you go.

Phyllis   He won't just turn up here, you know.

Angela   I know.

Phyllis   Not after last time. I made him perfectly aware. For all the thanks I got . . .

Angela   I know!

I saw little Jimmy's back.

Phyllis   *Little* Jimmy?

Angela   That's his car still outside. He must have got leave. Or be sick or hurt or something.

Phyllis   No. Jimmy's been back for a while. Eating his mom out of house and home, poor woman.

Angela   But he had a tour. For a year.

Phyllis   He did.

Angela   . . . That's a year?

Phyllis   As of last month. He's going back tonight.

Angela   Jesus . . .

Phyllis   Time does fly when . . . well, yeah.

Beat.

Angela   Give us a fag please, Mom.

Phyllis   Fuck off! I quit. I said I'd quit, I've quit.

This is me you're talking to, remember? I've got my patches, my gum. I might have a vapour lying around somewhere but after that . . .

Angela   I tried the gum. But, well . . .

You have to go somehow, don't you?

Phyllis   Somehow.

Angela   I can't believe that's been a year. I remember the day he left. Crystal clear. Him in his uniform. Looking so . . . handsome.

Phyllis   He looks tired now.

Angela   Don't we all. It's a shitty job.

Phyllis   For shitty people. Shitty, stupid people. That's who they scoop up.

Angela   Mom!

Phyllis   What?

Beat.

Angela   I've been keeping an ear out for their front door to say hi but . . . nothing. Probably packing though, if he's going back later.

Phyllis   Hark at you making all the effort, like he doesn't have your number.

Angela   Left my mobile, didn't I?

Phyllis   'Cause he's bothered to try and call you before? He's been back weeks.

Angela   No. It's just nice though, innit? To catch up and that. Even if it is brief. I've always had time for Jimmy.

Phyllis   Well, you should have popped round then, if you were that desperate to see him.

Angela   . . .

Phyllis   How many times do I have to tell you? Stay away. From the lot of 'em. They're no good. None of 'em.

Angela   Don't be daft. I'm not thinking in anyway. It's Jimmy.

Phyllis   Yes.

Angela   I just thought to say hey.

Plus, I could do with an extra pair of hands to go up to the flat with. And I know he'd help. He'd want to help.

Phyllis   An extra pair of hands for what?

Angela   Help me collect some stuff.

Phyllis   Stuff for what?

Angela   What do you mean 'stuff for what'? And stop shouting.

Phyllis   I'm not shouting. Don't get getting all sensitive 'cause you're feeling guilty.

Angela   Why would I be feeling guilty?

Phyllis   For grabbing your stuff? To go where with exactly?

Angela   Well, obviously not here.

Phyllis   You said you wanted one night. One.

Angela   Here, yes, but –

Phyllis   Now where are you planning on going?

Angela   Well, I can't go home, can I?

Phyllis   You can't go home?

Angela   How can I go home?

Phyllis   How can you not go home? You've got a babbie!

Angela   He hits me, Mom.

Beat.

Phyllis   You said you just needed one night. Which is why I allowed you to leave my granddaughter in that house. Now bring her here. Or go home.

Angela   He won't let me.

Scene Five

Angela *sits while* **Phyllis** *sorts through a bursting first-aid box.*

Phyllis   Right. Arnica, Ibuprofen . . . An anti-inflammatory . . . And you sleep with this on.

Angela   Ta.

Phyllis   Should get you looking a bit more presentable.

Angela   Jimmy ain't gonna care.

Phyllis   I care.

They're having a thing later for him. Next door.

Angela   Like a party?

Phyllis   No. Not a party. Just a bit of food, bit of drink, music and that. Before he has to set off. So you'd better hurry if you want him to do this first.

Angela   You going?

Phyllis   I was gonna.

Angela   I wouldn't have thought you'd bother. For Jimmy.

Phyllis   Just to show my face. His mom asked me to make something. Something for people to pick at. Was thinking of rustling up a few of them chocolate flapjacks you like. They're easy enough. Just for people to pick at. And cheaper than taking over a bottle. Although it isn't really. Is it? Not once you've bought all the ingredients. And then there's the time. And the mess. But still. You can't think about it like that. You wouldn't do anything if you thought about things like that, would you? Plus it gets me out the house. So I was gonna show my face. You thinking of coming?

Angela   No.

Phyllis   Good. Probably best. It's not worth the questions, again.

Angela   No.

Phyllis   But if you bring Demi back, I could take her. Cheer her up. She'd like that, wouldn't she?

Angela   Demi will be at her boyfriend's, Mom.

Phyllis   Oh?

Angela   She's never at home in the evenings. She has her own life, her own friends. I'm just . . . landlady.

Phyllis   Sounds familiar.

Angela   I signed up to Sky last month to try and keep her in a bit more. Twenty pounds a month –

Phyllis Twenty pounds?! You should have called me. Kid on the corner's selling the boxes for that. All channels.

Angela You said not to call.

Phyllis You said you didn't need me.

Beat.

Angela I'm gonna cancel it at the end of the trial. I just thought with the movie channels and what-not . . . Plus she likes them reality shows, but . . . Just ends up with him watching sport.

Phyllis He ain't gonna be there is he?

Angela He'll be down The Swan.

Phyllis Definite?

Angela *nods.*

Angela And if not, well that's why I'm asking Jimmy to come with.

Phyllis Jimmy ain't even family, it ain't even fair to ask.

Angela Who else is there to ask?

Phyllis *takes another prescribed painkiller.*

Phyllis Demi's got a boyfriend.

Angela *nods*

Phyllis Look at your face.

Angela So grown-up, it's scary.

Phyllis Yep.

Angela It scares me. When the hell did that happen?

Phyllis You're asking me?

What's he like?

Angela *shrugs*

Phyllis   Oh, I love it!

Angela   Leave off!

Phyllis   Taste of your own bloody medicine!

Angela   No . . .

Phyllis   And if she's mixing with the kind of toerags you used to mix with, you've the right to be scared!

Angela   He goes Bishop Visey.

Phyllis   Thank God one of us has taste!

Angela *and* **Phyllis** *share a laugh.*

Angela   Don't!

Phyllis   It's true!

Angela   Mine's not so bad.

Phyllis   Demi's father?

Angela   OK . . .

Phyllis   Makes this one look almost . . .

Angela   Alright, Mom!

And I don't remember Dad being so bad.

Phyllis   You probably don't remember much.

Angela   I remember when he'd watch TV, lay on the big three-seater in here and I'd sit behind his legs. Small enough to sit just there and play shop. With my plastic food and my plastic money. Using his legs as the counter.

And mainly I'd have to imagine people would come and buy food off me. And I'd do my little exchange with the air. But sometimes, when the breaks were on, Dad would turn round and buy something himself. And give me real money. Real coins. Ten p, twenty . . . fifty. A pound. You'd be in the kitchen. Cooking. And Dad would smuggle me money. And

say 'Shush, don't tell your mother'. And I'd have real money.
For tuck. Or brownies. I remember that.

Phyllis   You must remember the night he left. Me falling
down the stairs? Having to call the ambulance . . . ?

Angela   Not really.

Phyllis   You remember. You dialing 999 and showing off
about it for weeks. And when the ambulance came, who's all
beaming 'cause they're sitting up front with them? Sitting up
in the grown-up seats?

Angela   Yeah . . .

I remember it 'cause I was told. Everyone told me all that.
But I don't think I actually remember.

Phyllis   You were young.

Angela   And I remember he would lock me up in between
his legs when you were calling me for dinner. And be like . . .
'Go on then! Your mom's calling you. You'll get in trouble.'
And no matter how much I tried to escape I couldn't. And
the only way he'd let me go is if I shouted surrender and then
declared I was the weakest person in the whole wide world.

You didn't have such bad taste.

Beat.

Phyllis   You'll need to get in touch with the housing.

Angela   OK.

Phyllis   Get on a list.

Angela   Yes.

Phyllis   And then tonight?

Angela   I'll just go down to the police station. Tell them I'm
homeless. I'm with my daughter. Tell them I'm vulnerable.

Phyllis   You'll end up back at a refuge.

Angela   I've done it before. I'll manage.

Phyllis   Manage, she says.

Angela   I've done it before.

Phyllis   *I've* done it before. You were just there.

Angela   Yes. And I'll manage.

Phyllis   And Demi?

Beat.

Angela   Do I look OK ?

Phyllis   For Jimmy? You look fine.

Scene Six

Malachi *gets on the bus.* **Demi***'s sitting eating chips*

Malachi   What? You got no mouth?

Demi   I smiled innit?

Malachi   I swear you're following me.

Demi   I was on the bus first.

Malachi   So? What kinda proof is that? You've just clocked I'm always on here.

Demi   What? You're always on the bus.

Malachi   On this bus. At this time.

Demi   Well that's not true. You don't usually get on until 10.35.

Malachi   Huh?

Demi   Don't flatter yourself, I memorise bus routes.

Malachi   Well, ain't you cool?

Demi   I try.

Malachi   What are you doing on here?

Demi   I'm just taking a trip.

Malachi   What, on my bus? That's kinda dangerous still.

Demi   There's a grammar school round here somewhere, ain't there?

Malachi   Which one? King Edward's? Yeah, it's down that way somewhere. Think you have to catch the 16.

Demi   That's where that Hayley girl went. The one from Four Oaks.

Malachi   Ah, I read about her. Killed one girl?

Demi   Slashed her lover's new wife twenty-seven times across the face.

Malachi   Shit!

Extra-marital relationships for ya. That's why they're best left alone.

Demi   Imagine being that desperate and in love with someone that it drives you to do something like that.

Do you reckon he was grateful?

Malachi   Are you silly? She mercked his wife! Psychopath! She'd have got locked off.

Demi   Ugh, these are cold.

Want one?

She offers the chips to **Malachi**

Malachi   You're alright still. So where you going? And isn't it a little past your bedtime?

Demi   Coming from you?

Malachi   This ain't no open-top tourist thing, you know. It's the 11.

Demi   I know. *Your* bus.

Malachi   And don't you forget it.

It don't even go nowhere anyways. Especially at this hour. Just round and round through this dry place.

Demi   I don't care.

Malachi   Alright. Alright. I can spot a disappointed look anywhere. Not for no one else though. Just 'cause it's you. I'll give you your very own tour guide.

(*Putting on a voice.*) On the right-hand side we have Handsworth cricket ground. A very popular resort in summer, famous for its well-kept grass and West Indian food kitchen on the side.

Demi   Oh my God!

Malachi   Venture there at this hour mind and you're more likely to find crack addicts and runaways, along with one Rasta named Bob who reckons he's training for the Olympics.

Over to the left we have the student halls for UCE. A perfect selection of our future doctors, lawyers and bankers. If you look carefully you can probably see them philosophising away over herbal medicines in the back seat of that tinted-out Corsa.

As we continue down the hill we head towards *the* shopping destination of the rich and famous. Our very own 'ONE STOP'. *You* want it? ONE STOP has it. All under the *one* roof!

Demi   Sit down, will you? You're being loud!

Malachi   I'm sorry, madam. What was that? You can't see for all the clouds? Well if you want to sit up front with me you should have just asked.

Demi   I'm ignoring you!

Malachi   Dudley Zoo? No, not on this route, madam. However, if you're interested we do sell discount tickets. You just have a word with the driver at the end of the tour. Flash him that winning smile of yours and he may even knock a few extra quid off.

Demi   You think you're so funny.

Malachi   And yet you're laughing.

Demi   I'm not laughing. I'm . . . humouring you.

Malachi   Good enough. Especially after the week I've had.

Demi   Tough week, Mr Tour Guide?

Malachi   Just kinda nice being listened to.

Demi   Why?

Malachi   . . . My cousin Tubz, yeah, who's like a brother to me, isn't even trying to hear anything I have to say at the minute. Ignoring my calls, airing my messages . . .

Demi   With regard to what?

Malachi   Some drama innit? It's long.

Demi   We've time.

Malachi   A bit of mix-up kicked off and somehow it's my fault. Me? I couldn't even find trouble if I went looking for it.

Demi   I find that hard to believe. I mean you grated on me when I first met you.

Malachi   And yet you keep coming back for more.

Demi   Seriously. People don't get vex for no reason.

Malachi   People don't piss off their own. Not when that's all they've got. Why would I do that? Does that make any sense to you?

Demi   You have a brother.

Malachi   Who's a kid. And not even mine, fully. He spends his weekends more with his dad. Tubz is . . . It's always been the two of us. And, yeah, recently he's getting a bit more gassed, but . . .

Demi   I'm just saying there's never smoke without –

Malachi   What happened to your face?

Demi   What?

Malachi   It looks swollen.

Demi   Nah, it's your eyesight, bab. Must fail you at night.
You should stock up on carrots.

Malachi   Don't snap at me 'cause you're getting beaten by
your Mini-Cooper-driving boyfriend.

Demi   Do you really think any man could disrespect me like
that?

Malachi   You're really up on this female independence shit!
You a lesbian? I mean, it's cool if you is.

Demi   Right . . .

Malachi   And if ever you'd want me to watch . . . or join in
even . . .

Demi   I think you best open a window and cool yourself.

Malachi   Nah, I'm ramping. You cool?

Demi   . . . Yeah.

Malachi   And your face?

Demi   Seriously! Carrots.

Malachi   Alright!

Demi   So, how come's you're on the bus already? You don't
usually get on till Stockland Green.

Malachi   I knew you was on it!

Demi   Excuse me?

Malachi   Watching mans like cooked food.

Demi   If that makes you happy.

Malachi   Nah, I was at my bredrin's down Grove Lane.
Bunning budha, having a one drink . . .

Demi   Wow. You're so cool.

Malachi   What, you telling me you don't smoke?

Demi   Hell no. Smoking's for idiots.

Malachi   How would you know if you've never done it before?

Demi   Who said I'd never done it?

Malachi   You look like a good girl.

Demi   You just seemed shocked that I was telling you I didn't smoke.

Malachi   Yeah, well. I changed my mind. You look like a book girl.

Demi   A book girl?

Malachi   A girl that reads books and shit.

Demi   Funnily enough, I managed to crack that code. As complicated as it was.

Malachi   You live in Handsworth then?

Demi   Where?

Malachi   Round these sides?

Demi   Nah, I don't really know this side of Birmingham. It's nice though.

Malachi   Nice?

Demi   Yeah, the park and that. And the houses here. It's pretty.

Malachi   True say we're just skimming the surface I can see how you'd think that. So what are you doing round here?

Demi   I get off way back there, by the hospital. There's this chip shop I'd read about online and it's good. Has its own Facebook page so I go to it. Get a cone or a scallop with extra vinegar and then walk down to the next stop opposite the prison and wait for the next bus which usually comes about ten-oh-five.

Malachi   Well look at you, living the dream!

Demi   Funny.

Malachi   You do that every night?

Demi   Why not?

Malachi   Ya dad needs to teach you about finding your yard?

Beat.

Where you even from, Miss 'I've never heard of Handsworth'?

Demi   Kings Heath.

Malachi   Posh gal!

Demi   If you say so.

Malachi   How old are you?

Demi   Guess.

Malachi   Seventeen?

Demi *makes game-show noise for an incorrect answer.*

Malachi   You're not that much older than me.

Demi   How old are you?

Malachi   Guess.

Demi   Twelve?

Malachi   Why be like that?

Demi   You love it.

Malachi   You think?

Demi   I know.

Malachi   When am I gonna get your number?

Demi   What do you need my number for?

Malachi   Well one day I might be running late and miss that ten-oh-five bus, and then who am I gonna talk to?

Demi   How's about 'Tubz'? Or one of your other imaginary friends.

Malachi   Yeah yeah.

Demi   Where do you go every night at this hour? Girl's house?

Malachi   Would that make you sad?

Demi   Do you ever just answer a question?

Malachi   Coming from you?!

Sorry. Go again.

Demi   You linking a girl?

Malachi   I wish.

Demi   What? That you had a girl?

Malachi   Ha! Nah, I'm going work, innit?

Demi   Where do you work?

Malachi   One factory up by Cadbury's World.

Demi   And you're so young? That don't sound right.

Malachi   Who said I'm young?

Demi   I'm telling you you're young.

Malachi   Don't watch mans.

Demi   You've changed your tune, and I only watch myself.

Malachi   Do you really have a boyfriend?

Demi   Kinda.

Malachi   And does he really drive a Mini Cooper?

Demi   It's been known.

Malachi   What's he do?

Demi   You're coming like police?

Malachi   Just showing an interest.

Demi   This and that.

Malachi   Oh. I understand! He's one of those geezers. You're one of many, I'll tell you that from now.

Beat.

Nah, you just must be too good for him though, really.

Demi *smiles*

Malachi   Ha! I proper like you, you know?

Demi   Boys like you probably like a lot of girls.

Malachi   Nah, I don't even mean like that. Like, I've proper got time for you. You're cool.

Demi   Thanks. You're not so bad yourself.

Malachi   Gee, thanks.

Demi   Take my number.

Malachi   Yeah?

Demi   And one bell me so I've got yours.

Malachi   Ah, I ain't even got creds richa now.

Demi *laughs*

Malachi   What? You laughing 'cause I don't have credit.

Demi   I'm laughing 'cause you've got a pay-as-you-go phone.

Malachi   I'll get some. Tomorrow.

Demi   Cool.

Malachi   Where you getting off?

Demi   Might not?

Malachi   What, you just gonna stay on?

Demi This bus takes me right to my door. Why would I get off?

Malachi Well, now I'm more thinking why would you get on?

Demi If I was at home I'd be doing the same thing. Sat. Just in front of a telly.

Malachi Exactly.

Demi I don't really watch TV.

Malachi Do you know how long it takes to do the whole route? You'll be on here –

Demi Two hours, twenty-five minutes.

Malachi Oh. Is that it?

Demi It's kinda cool still. Kills time. And you see all sorts.

Malachi Like what? Mans?

Demi Maybe.

Malachi Thought you had a geezer.

Demi I said kinda.

Malachi Ah yeah, 'cause he effs out on you, innit?

Demi You know what –

Malachi Did he get you a Valentine's present?

Demi . . . No. We're . . . well . . . no . . .

Malachi Wasteman!

Demi Did you get your girlfriend a Valentine's present?

Malachi Now that would be telling.

Demi You just make sure you treat her right, 'cause my ex . . . Man. I would have done anything for him and yet still . . . it's like it wasn't enough . . .

Malachi So he's your ex now?

Demi   I don't know what he is.

Beat.

Malachi *pulls out a packet of crisps from his pocket.*

Malachi   Monster Munch?

Demi   I'm cool.

Malachi   Well, if you're just circling and I'm trekking all the way to Bourneville we can just chill, innit? Any decent music on that? (*Indicating her iPod.*)

Demi   It's alright still. Yours?

Malachi   Mainly Hip-hop.

Demi   We'll listen to mine.

They share headphones while **Demi** *finds a song. Lights fade.*

Scene Seven

Angela *enters. Switching on the light, she sees* **Phyllis** *sitting in the dark.*

Phyllis   Sorted?

Angela   Shit!

Hello.

Phyllis   Just took a little longer than expected?

Angela   A tad.

Phyllis   Are you drunk?

Angela   No!

Phyllis   You're drunk!

Angela   *You're* drunk! Sitting in the dark like a weirdo!

Phyllis   And where's Demi?

Angela   At her boyfriend's! I told you.

Phyllis   She's staying there again?

Angela   I figured best not to disrupt her.

Phyllis   You said . . .

Angela   What?

Phyllis   How are you getting into the hostel without her?

Angela   Who cares! I've bloody done it, Mom! I've done it! Got my stuff. Gone.

Phyllis   You took ages. I was thinking all sorts.

Angela   I had to say thank you.

Phyllis   You what?

Angela   To Jimmy. You were right. He ain't family so . . .

I said I'd treat him to a quick bite to eat. Up the Stratford Road. Nothing . . . And a pint.

Phyllis   Just the one?

Angela   We weren't that long.

Phyllis   Tell that to his mom sat next door waiting for him. You said you'd be an hour.

Angela   Well, he's back now.

Phyllis   Now he's missed his party.

Angela   And he's gonna pop round in a second to say goodbye properly. If you were worried . . . Or you just pop round! It's not so late. Though you'll probably be the only one there.

Phyllis   I was the only one there.

Angela   Belle of the ball!

Jimmy used to call me that when we were younger. We'd go to any party and he'd say, 'You're the belle of the ball.'

Twat!

Is that Disney?

Phyllis   No.

Angela   I reminded him about that tonight and he went bright red. It was so cute.

Phyllis   Well, as long as you had a good night.

Angela   And kinda interesting . . . He's never got with anyone. After all these years. After thinking I was . . . I don't know. Just kinda find that interesting. Really.

Phyllis   He is away for months at a time with work.

Angela   Sure. Argh! I've done it! I feel like I could do anything. I'm capable of anything!

Do you know what else he said?

Phyllis   Go on.

Angela   That he was jealous of me. Said no matter what anyone tried to say I should remember I was doing what I wanted. Always. And that made me lucky.

Phyllis   Jesus Christ.

Angela   It's nice that, ain't it? That he sees that in me. He really sees me.

Phyllis   You changed your outfit?

Angela   Huh?

Phyllis   To go and collect your stuff . . .

Angela   No.

Phyllis   You got changed.

Angela   Oh no, just . . . my jeans were too tight. For all the lifting and that.

Phyllis   You can see every lump and bump in that dress.

Angela It's not a dress. It's a jumper.

Phyllis That you wear with just tights?

Angela That I wear with leggings.

Phyllis Leggings? Very fashionable.

Angela . . . Thanks. Shall I make us a tea?

Phyllis Not at this hour. I wouldn't sleep.

Angela It's really not that late.

Phyllis But still.

Angela But still . . . I might have one though. It's proper dropped tonight.

Phyllis I can imagine you're cold.

Angela Well, I've got more stuff now . . . And I found Demi's christening bracelet!

Phyllis Oh nice.

Angela And my costume from when I was picked to play Queen of the Sea in the school show. The green dress?

Phyllis You kept that?

Angela After all the work you put in? It's covered in sequins and gems, all hand-stitched. An hour every day before dinner.

Phyllis For two whole weeks.

Angela And I was responsible for threading the needles and tying the knots . . .

Phyllis And you didn't even bloody wear it after all that.

Angela 'Cause we left.

Phyllis Left?

Angela After they let you out of the hospital . . . We had to leave.

Phyllis Only for two weeks.

Angela Until Dad left. I'd got a nurse to test me on my lines as well. Mrs Richardson kept saying whilst she was proud of how brilliantly I'd memorised both my part and everyone else's for my cues, it wasn't completely necessary for me to mouth the other lines alongside. I had to practise that bit.

Phyllis Drama queen from birth.

Angela Not that anyone will ever know. Miss picks me. You break your hip. And Laura bloody Tinald gets recast as my part.

Beat

Can't believe Jimmy's leaving tonight. That's . . . crap.

Phyllis Yeah.

Angela He hates being in the army as well. He was saying. They don't give a shit about you. Jimmy's words. It sounds . . .

Phyllis Quite.

Angela Drives some people to run away. He was saying. They need to just escape. Just disappear into the night. I can see that.

Phyllis I'll bet.

Angela Regain some sort of control. I can see why you'd want to do that.

Phyllis I bought the flapjacks back, should you want to take some with you.

Angela And we were laughing about the time school took us to that beach. After SATs. Up by Rhyl. Do you remember that trip? He tried to kiss me that summer. Cheeky shit! In this little hidden cove while the other kids were rock climbing. And he was saying tonight, if ever we went back there . . . if ever he took me back there, to that place, our special place,

he'd try again. Properly this time. And I was saying I might
let him.

Phyllis   Oh dear God, give me strength.

Angela   I want him to do it here. Now. Tonight. Make it . . .
official tonight.

Phyllis   Make what official?

Angela   He's had to rush back 'cause his mom was getting
mardy, but he'll be here in a sec. I'm just gonna say.

Phyllis   Say what?

Angela   He shouldn't go back to work if he's not happy. Not
for a year. That's not right. He should just explain.

Phyllis   What?

Angela   Everyone should live exactly as they want to.

Phyllis   Did you make it to the police station?

Angela   It's funny though, isn't it?

Phyllis   You don't want to be walking the streets at this
hour.

Angela   I'm here with all my stuff packed. He's there with
all his. Both with nowhere to go.

Phyllis   Don't go putting ideas in people's heads.

Angela   Talking about Rhyl and hating work and being
spontaneous . . . ?

Phyllis   You're in la-la land!

Angela   He wants to leave. He wants to run away. To
Wales. With . . . me. He's practically said it.

Phyllis   Only he hasn't. Why don't you pull your head out
the clouds for once?!

Angela   He'll be here in a second.

Phyllis   Grow up!

Angela So we can talk then.

Phyllis You're a mom!

Angela Demi's fine!

Phyllis Is she? You don't bloody know!

Angela She'll be fine, better than fine. This is all gonna be perfect.

Phyllis And in the meantime . . . ? Whilst you're building your dream? You leaving her with him?

Angela He's her dad.

Phyllis Not properly.

Angela As good as. And he loves her.

Phyllis He loved you.

Angela Fine. It's a risk! There, are you happy? I'm taking a massive risk. But I'd rather that than have her here with you.

Phyllis What?

Angela I don't want her here in this house with you. You're polluted. You'll infect her. I'm sorry, but it's true. I bring my daughter up to know about living and loving and being alive and you . . . you're not 'safe', you're . . . nothing.

Beat.

Jimmy will be here in a second.

Phyllis To whisk you away?

Angela I'll be out your hair. Permanently.

He said he'd stop by . . .

For sure.

Phyllis Then let's wait. For your Prince Charming, let's just wait.

Scene Eight

Demi's *sitting behind* **Malachi**, *leaning over while he's texting*

Demi   Alisha, eh?

Malachi   Did you not hear how curiosity killed the cat?

Demi   Yeah, but having nine lives and all you can afford to take risks.

Malachi   You a risk-taker then?

Beat.

You don't have to be embarrassed to say you're jealous.

Demi   I've got nothing to be jealous of.

Malachi   You're right still. Alisha's just any girl.

Demi   No, 'cause me and you ain't . . . anything.

Malachi   Yet.

Demi   Ha!

Malachi   How comes you never even belled me back yesterday?

Demi   I didn't recognise the number.

Malachi   Then what was the point of giving me your digits, yeah, if you know you don't answer foreign numbers? You may as well have just took mine.

Demi   True.

Malachi   Are you always this difficult?

Demi   With what?

Malachi   With men?

Demi   Ah, you think you're a man?

Malachi   You know what . . . ?

Demi   What?

Malachi . . . How did your ex even get you?

Demi *smiles. Then notices something out the window.*

Demi Ha! Look! My leisure centre! You see those swimming baths over there? That's where I had my first kiss. Round the side with Thomas McDonnell.

Malachi Sounds like a white-boy name.

Demi We went swimming club together. I was fourteen and basically everyone I ever knew had started kissing boys from time. Who am I kidding, most of the girls in my class were lying down with boys by this point and I was just getting my first kiss. But I didn't care 'cause I proper fancied him. Most of my mates' first kisses were with guys from the boys' school at the school disco. Drunk on the twenty-twenty that they'd managed to sneak in, in Panda Pops bottles!

Malachi You rebels.

Demi Then my dad came to pick me up early and –

Malachi What? Caught you? Ha! No way! What did he say?

Demi It's closed down now. They're rebuilding it. Do you know a kid drowned in there? Slipped and banged his head on the top diving board before falling off. Can you imagine that? Ridiculous. Like something from an Ian McEwan book.

Malachi I don't really read, still.

Demi But imagine, something awful like that happens and all memories can be erased with a clean slate. Fresh start. It's perfect.

Malachi Did your dad go mental for finding you with a boy?

Demi My dad is mental. Period.

Malachi Really?

Demi Maybe. But no one gets on with their parents, right?

Malachi I don't know. Me and my mom are pretty tight.

Demi   Yeah?

Malachi   She works a lot and I have to help out where I can but . . . She taught me how to play chess when I was ten. On this board my auntie brought back from St Lucia. All the little pieces delicately carved out of some sort of stone. All polished and kinda looking more like an ornament than a game, but still. The fact that she taught me when I was so young I figure means she thinks I'm pretty ace. Has always thought I was pretty brilliant. I'm just saying : . . . And we keep that board in the living room on the side piece in front of all mine and my brothers' school photos and certificates and this one random dry photo of Princess Diana I think she cut from a magazine. And whenever we're both in on our own together with a bit of time we continue this same game we've been playing for months. And that's how it goes. It's mine and her thing.

You'd love her.

Demi   Oh yeah? What about your dad?

Malachi   Same. Thick as thieves. Or at least we could be, if I knew what he looked like.

Kinda common nowadays though, right?

Demi   Doesn't stop it hurting.

Malachi   It only hurts if you let it. And how can you let it? There's just too much to be grateful for.

Demi   Big words from someone who's just lost their only friend.

Malachi   And then I find you.

Beat.

Demi   You wanted to kick me when we first met.

Malachi   No!

Demi   You said that. I remember specifically.

Malachi   I wouldn't have said no such thing.

Demi   You say anything like that again –

Malachi   I'll let you kick me! Wherever you want.

He shifts legs.

Not there though . . .

No! Fuck it! There! For even saying it!

I don't know what I was thinking.

Demi   Nor do I.

Malachi   I'm sorry.

I could never hurt you. I would never hurt you.

Demi   . . . Snap.

Malachi   I got goosebumps you saying that to me then.

Demi   Yeah?

Malachi   Yeah.

Demi   Good.

Malachi   So come on. You and your folks.

Demi's *phone rings.*

Demi   Shit! Sorry.

Malachi   No, it's cool.

You gonna get that?

Demi   Erm . . . no. No, it's not . . .

Malachi   I don't care. I can just go back to messaging
Alisha or something.

Demi   Ha!

Malachi   Or not. Or never again!

But, for real. If it's important. I'll wait. I won't even eavesdrop
or anything.

Demi It's cool. I just . . .

She receives a text.

Malachi Yeah?

Demi . . .

Demi Isn't this your stop?

Malachi I can get off the next one.

Demi No . . . just . . .

Malachi What? What's wrong?

Demi Sometimes I think I can tell you anything.

Malachi Dems, is this about your dad?

Demi No.

Malachi What goes on him at home?

Demi Nothing. Don't ever really see him.

Malachi But you do get on?

Demi Oi. You best get up from now before you miss this stop and end up walking a mission in the rain trying to cuss me!

Malachi Fine! I'm gonna bell you on my break, though!

Demi Yeah, yeah.

Malachi Make sure you answer.

Demi Hurry!

Malachi Make sure!

Demi OK, OK!

Malachi In a bit.

Demi See ya.

Blackout.

Scene Nine

Angela *and* **Phyllis** *are both sitting in silence, exhausted.*

Beat.

Phyllis   Gonna learn Arabic.

Ordered a Linguaphone set from off the internet. Yet to arrive but . . .

No one would expect it, would they? Me speaking a whole new language, and that language being Arabic. It won't be easy. It's a completely different alphabet, but it's not about that. That's not why you should choose to do anything, is it?

There's these two Moroccan women that enjoy a filter coffee in the café at ASDA. They sit at the back and natter away to themselves, every Monday. I treat myself to a slice of lemon drizzle and an Earl Grey after doing the weekly shop. And sometimes I think how nice it would be to be able to join in with them

Only if I had something to say . . . had an opinion. Not for the sake of it. I just thought that would be nice.

And it's important to keep learning.

And it doesn't bother anyone. Doesn't hurt anyone. But with you . . . it's always extreme. Like with the swing at the bottom of the garden. And who had to test drive it? Muggins here. All hunky-dory at first, swinging higher and higher, until I could see over the roofs of the houses at the back. And then over the treetops behind them. And then higher still until I could just make out a bit of green behind that. A hilly field way back there. With animals on it. Horses, I think. Right just at the back of here. I could see them dotted on the grass and I thought . . . what the heck are horses doing around here? And then I realised there's a whole bloody world out there that I know nothing about. And I'm so high looking out at it. With the wind in my face, and then smack. Swing legs come clean out the ground and I'm on the concrete path with two scuffed knees and elbows and a grazed chin.

Are you listening?

Angela   You fell off the swing.

Phyllis   You don't go nosying for greener pastures.

Angela   . . . That's not what that means.

Phyllis   You be happy with your lot. That's what that means. 'Cause look what happens?

Jimmy left. Couldn't even say goodbye.

And I said, didn't I? I did say. Stay away. From the lot of them. They're not worth it. None. To be with these men it's like you've got to give them Kryptonite and just pray they never use it against you.

Well. At least you saw it. You see. Properly now. What they're like. Hey, Ange?

Angela   . . . Yes. You were right.

Phyllis   And was that so hard?

I'll get the kettle on.

Lights fade.

Scene Ten

Malachi's *sitting at the back of the bus, waiting expectantly.* **Demi** *enters.*

Malachi   Rare! I proper didn't think you'd show, you know?

Demi   Didn't think I'd show? You've been belling off my line all up until now?

Malachi   Yeah, well, you could have been blagging. Saying you're here and you ain't. It's late still.

Demi   Not much later than when we're usually on the bus.

Malachi   Yeah, but it's after eleven. Drunkard's time!

Demi   Well that's cool I've got a strapping man to protect me! Hmm . . . on second thoughts maybe I'll just sit near the fire exit!

Malachi   Wrenk!

You missed me?

Demi   Missed you? I don't know you!

Malachi   I've proper been thinking about you all week, you know?

Demi   Well, that'll explain the incessant ringing!

Malachi   You don't have to answer the calls if you don't want to speak.

Demi   You look like the type of boy that would cry easily!

Malachi   You dickhead!

Demi   Don't worry, it's cool! I know loads of girls who love a guy in touch with his feelings! None of them are from Birmingham but, you know, we have good train links now, and what with the coach doing one-pound tickets there's really no excuses!

Malachi   I'm starting to think I preferred you better when you didn't used speak.

Demi   Well that's not true! 'Tubz' couldn't give you banter the way I can give you banter.

Malachi   It's not banter I'm after with you though!

Demi   Oi! You save that sweet-boy talk for one of your flexes.

Malachi   Of course, 'cause I'm not your type still. Gal like you likes bad man!

Demi   No!

Malachi   Well then, give me a chance!

Demi *smiles.*

Malachi   Alright. I didn't think I'd have to draw this out. I mean this is low, but if it's bad men you're after, listen to this. This one time, yeah, times were hard. I mean, proper hard. Before we had words like 'credit crunch' to define it! Mans like me hadn't eaten in time and was needing a new pair of boots for work, innit?

Demi   Go on.

Malachi   So one day I'm just thinking, fuck it! Fuck the system! I jumped on the bus dropped in a one twenty-pence piece and said 'Next stop please', sat upstairs and stayed on that bus all the way to Bourneville!

Demi   Ha! You knob!

Malachi   But you fancy me more now, innit? Now you know I'm not a law-abiding citizen?

Demi   Is that your big criminal activity?

Malachi   'Fraid so! I beg you don't tell no one! I'm so ashamed! Sometimes I find it difficult to sleep at night.

Demi   Funny!

So how comes I'm hearing you were about when some mans rushed one geezer in town?

Malachi   You know them mans?

Demi   I know of them.

Malachi   What do you know?

Demi   That I should stay away?

Malachi   Dunno about that . . . I reckon they'd be right up your street based on what you's telling me 'bout your ex.

Demi   . . . Nah. They're not for me.

Malachi   And who is for you?

Demi   How do you know them?

Malachi   Ah, they just ride with my cousin still, Tubz. Not really my friends. I ain't got time for no gang life! Got shit to do, innit?

Demi   But you were there that day?

Malachi   As an observer. One of many. It happened ra in the middle of the Bullring, innit?!

Demi   What happened?

Malachi   The geezer got wet up.

Demi   Wet?

Malachi   Like, stabbed him.

Demi   Oh.

Malachi   Them mans are nutty. No one told them to do no such thing. They were just supposed to scare the geezer.

Demi   How comes?

Malachi   'Cause the geezer did my cousin something so it was like a revenge thing. This geezer's people tried to beat up Tubz so then Tubz's bredrins rushed him back.

Demi   You?

Malachi   Nah, I stayed well out of it. In town? That's bait. Hence why he's screwing with me now like some little bitch.

Demi   How did you lot know that guy was gonna be in town?

Malachi   The geezer went my school. Dartmouth. We used to ride back in the day but just kinda lost touch. But when I

heard what happened to Tubz I said let me link him and ask
him why. I knew it wouldn't have been him involved
personally. I told Tubz and he was like, screw that, he's going
there too, with mans. I was meant to meet him outside the
food quarter. On the ground floor? But I fell back. I couldn't
go when all them lot were gonna rock up. I knew what Tubz
would be on. And it's not like he'd need my help. He had an
army, and besides, technically I'd done my bit.

Demi   By setting him up?

Malachi   Hey. You don't know the ins and outs of it. The
geezer was out of line really for not just controlling his people.
Besides, you're gonna play with fire . . . well, he deserved to
get burnt.

Demi   He thought you were friends.

Malachi   So. He ain't my blood.

Demi   He was somebody's.

Malachi   What? Yours?

Demi   He's my boyfriend.

Malachi   What?

Demi   You heard.

Malachi   You know what. I suggest you don't talk to me
any more.

Demi   He's getting on the bus at the next stop.

Malachi   What?

Demi   Him and his friends.

Malachi   Are you taking the piss?

Demi   Just to talk it out.

Malachi   Are you dumb?

Demi   Stop anything escalating.

Malachi   You fucking . . .

Demi   It's no worse then what you did.

Malachi   But you're . . . We're . . .

Demi   Friends? I'm sorry.

Blackout.

Scene Eleven

Angela *is sitting almost in a foetal position on the sofa.* **Phyllis** *paces, despite difficulty.*

Phyllis   We get her in a cab. We get her here.

Angela   . . . Right.

Phyllis   I don't know where your head's been this week, I really don't. It's like he knocked the common sense out of ya. But it's all worked out. For the best. It all came good, in the end. Could have come good a year ago, if you'd have listened, but . . . I won't go on.

Ow, this back.

Angela   . . . Thanks.

Phyllis   You'll stay in the attic, and you'll straighten out the spare room for Demi.

Angela   She can just kip in with me.

Phyllis   Nonsense. There's spare linen in the airing cupboard –

Angela   Honestly . . .

Phyllis   Smell it first though 'cause I want it fresh, otherwise . . .

Angela   That's just silly.

Phyllis   Demi likes her sheets to smell fresh, like you used to. Spoilt, but . . .

Angela   We're not gonna be staying that long.

Phyllis   It's best she's comfortable. And you won't know how long you'll be staying.

Angela   To be adding to the laundry . . . ? That's just not necessary.

Phyllis   You can't know what's gonna be necessary, at the minute.

Angela   It's just a roof.

Phyllis   It's not.

Angela   Until I get back on my feet.

Angela   I just need Demi settled.

Phyllis   She can be settled here.

Angela   She can be. But that's not the point.

Phyllis   Then what is the point?

Angela   For us to do it as a unit.

Phyllis   Exactly.

Angela   As a mother and daughter unit.

Phyllis   As a family unit. Why are you trying to exclude me?

Angela   I'm not. But this isn't about you.

Phyllis   Of course it's about me. This is my house.

Angela   And I've said thank you. But I need to do this on my own.

Phyllis   'Said thank you'?

Angela   What did you want?

Phyllis   What do you think I want?

Angela   For us to move in permanently? Is that what you want?

Phyllis   Do you have any other option?

Angela   Ha! That is what you want?!

Phyllis   Does Demi . . . ?

Angela   To have me and Demi holed up in this cell, with you? Seeing me miserable, me humiliated for you to have someone to play host to?

Phyllis   It's about Demi's safety.

Angela   It's about no such thing. You would rather have Demi walk in here, and see me like this. A failure. The one thing I've managed to shelter her from, the one thing I've managed to protect her from, you can't wait to destroy.

Phyllis   Don't be dramatic.

Angela   She'd never forgive me.

Phyllis   For being his punchbag?

Angela   For being crap enough to let him hit me in the first place. What kind of woman would do that?

Beat.

Phyllis   You blame me?

Angela   I'm sorry?

Phyllis   For your father shoving me down the stairs? You blame me?

Angela   . . . No.

Phyllis   For having him shatter my insides?

Angela   I never said that.

Phyllis   You blame me for the thumping and the bursting of every inch of my skin? And you blamed me?!

Angela   No! God forbid! You're a victim, we get it! We heard!

Phyllis   I need my pills.

Angela   Oh, here we go.

Phyllis   Pass me my pills.

Angela   Don't change the subject!

Phyllis   I'm hot. I can't breathe . . .

Angela   How convenient!

Phyllis   I need my pills, Angel.

Angela   I'd never felt so ashamed. For all the fighting and screaming and letting him chuck you around like a rag doll.

Phyllis   Please –

Angela   Are you getting hot again?

Phyllis   I can't . . .

Angela   Feeling weak?

Phyllis   . . .

Angela   Like you can't breathe?

Phyllis   I can't.

Angela   Fine! You want your pills! Here! Have them. The lot.

*She takes **Phyllis**'s painkillers and shoves them down her throat. It's never certain if it's too many.*

Angela   And your stick. And your shoes. And whatever else you need to maintain this sad soulless solitary so-called life! You're a mom. You're supposed to be brilliant.

No, swallow. Them all. You wanted them. You got them. Making out like I don't know how to look after my own daughter. Like I need any advice from you! You! Of all people, you! Look at you! You can't even look after yourself!

Blackout.

Scene Twelve

Demi (*off*)   Nan! Nan!

Demi *enters, her face tear-stained.* **Angela** *is sitting in her mom's chair.* **Phyllis** *is lying on the sofa. Her face seems to light up at* **Demi**'s *voice.*

Beat.

Angela   Hiya, love.

Demi   Hiya, Mom.

Angela   You're out and about late.

Demi   . . . I was just passing and saw the light on.

Thought I'd say hi.

Angela   Ah, bless ya. Nan's having a lie-down though, bab. Not feeling to well.

Demi   Oh right.

Angela   Drugged up to the eyeballs, as usual. I try and tell her. But does she listen?

You OK?

Demi   Yes. Yes, thanks.

You?

Angela   Oh, you know me. Surviving.

You've changed your hair.

Demi   No.

Angela   I mean you have . . .

Demi   Oh, this hair? Yeah . . . Just ran the straighteners through it.

Angela   Looks nice.

Demi   Thanks.

Angela   And your top . . . It's nice.

Demi   It's yours.

Angela   I know.

Still. Suits ya. You look . . . good.

Demi   I only came round 'cause . . .

Angela   I know. This is where we all come . . . Don't we, Mom?

When we feel like crap. This house just invites it.

Demi   How are feeling, Nan? You OK?

Phyllis *nods slowly.*

Demi   Shall I get your cushion?

Phyllis   No.

Demi   You're alright?

Phyllis *smiles*

Angela   She's fine. And couldn't take any more painkillers anyhow. Not safe.

Shame.

Demi   Is she alright?

Angela   It's only her back, bab. Course she is. She just needs to rest it off.

Here! Look what Mom picked it up down the market the other day. Bet you'd love something like this. Reaches right across the room. We wouldn't even have to get off the couch during a movie night! Remember? We've got Sky, Dems. We ain't even done that yet. Fancy it? Just the two of us? Or your boy, if you wanted.

Or is that not . . . no longer a thing.

Phyllis *reaches out and takes* **Demi***'s hand.*

Angela   Well, forget about him. His loss anyhow. A stunning girl like you? You'll be snapped up in no time. And him? He'll . . . well, he'll . . .

Well, who cares.

Demi   I meant to stay away, Nan, I promise. I just . . . I don't know. I thought . . .

Angela   Demi!

Demi   I promise you from now on I'll stay right away. I promise. 'Cause . . .

I properly see now.

Angela   Dems!

Demi   They're no good. None of them.

Angela   No. You don't do that. Punish yourself for one little mistake, for ever. 'Cause that's all it is. A mistake. You move on. OK ?

Beat.

Is there anyone else you've got your eye on?

Demi   . . .

Angela   See, Mom! Like mother like daughter after all, eh?

Demi *shrugs*

Angela   And we'll never know what he's like, will we, Mom? Nowhere near cool enough.

Are you OK ?

Demi   I just want . . .

Phyllis   What do you want, bab?

Demi   To go home.

Angela   Then that's what we'll do.

The End.